Catching the Light

Suzanne Edgar is a versatile Canberra writer. She has published successful short fiction, essays, and literary criticism in addition to much well-received poetry. Suzanne was on the editorial staff of the *Australian Dictionary of Biography*, to which she has contributed fifty-three articles. Her poems have been included in *Best Australian Poems*, Black Inc., 2004, 2005, 2011, 2012, 2015.

Her short fiction: *Canberra Tales* (with Seven Writers), Penguin, 1988, reprinted as *The Division of Love*, Penguin, 1995; *Counting Backwards*, UQP, 1991.

Her poetry books: *The Painted Lady* (Indigo, 2006, reprinted 2007); *The Love Procession*, Ginninderra Press, 2012 (both books were shortlisted for the ACT Writing & Publishing Awards); *Still Life* (Picaro Press, 2012).

Suzanne Godwin Edgar

Catching the Light

Thanks

Each of these people, dear husband and friends, was generous in helping me to prepare *Catching the Light* for publication: Peter, as always, with wise commentary and technical support; Rose Mawby with sound advice; and Lyn Millar with proofreading. Michael Thorley, Melinda Smith and Martin Dolan, colleagues at the Mull & Fiddle, have been my best and fairest critics in their first reading of new poems. I am grateful, too, to Darryl Bennet and the late John Beston for their steadfast encouragement over many years.

For my father, Charles E. Blake Godwin

Catching the Light
ISBN 978 1 76041 736 9
Copyright © text Suzanne Godwin Edgar 2019
Front cover photo: Peter Edgar
Author photo: Judith Crispin

First published 2019 by
GINNINDERRA PRESS
PO Box 3461 Port Adelaide 5015
www.ginninderrapress.com.au

Contents

This healing light	9
Starshine: double vision	11
Klimt in the courtyard: woman in gold	12
Compositions in a cold climate	13
Tonal effect, driving home	14
Metaphor	15
Resurrection	16
Pictures at a gallery	17
Sketch	18
Millais does Shakespeare in winter	19
Silent film	20
A glutton, on reading Szymborska's poems	21
His mother's voice	22
Natural bigamists	23
The fatal interruption, imagined	24
Where two walls meet	27
The Cross in winter	29
Change and dismay	30
Watercolour sketch, Canberra	31
Phasmida the stick-insect woman	32
Basement blues	33
Who do you think you are?	34
Against incineration	35
Country church	36
Dead flies have been trapped	37
The visitor eats, New Year's Eve	38
Happy? Why would you be?	39

True minds — 41

- True minds — 43
- A man — 44
- In praise of easy days — 45
- A correspondence — 46
- *Aimez-vous* Chekhov? — 47
- Sonnet for the second thought — 48
- Refuge — 49
- The haircut — 50
- Edge — 51
- Something is about to happen — 52
- Creature comforts — 53
- Signs of life — 54
- Summertime — 55
- The gift — 56
- The red chalk drawing — 57
- Lament — 58

Watchers — 59

- In two minds — 61
- A reverie — 62
- The temptation — 63
- Wishful Thinking — 64
- After fifty years — 65
- Closing the gap — 66
- Watchers — 67
- The fragrance of lemons — 68
- The silence — 70
- Zara going home — 71
- Your roses — 72
- Interwoven — 73
- The fever suite — 74
- Suspended — 76

For want of a spoon	77
Endgame	79
Night watch	80
A silver teaspoon	81
The force	82
He was an entertainment	83
A hundred times	84
A popular song, 1930s	85
Water sleekly falls	87
Sun on my back	89
Bush walk	90
Reflections, Jerrabomberra	91
The Chigaree	92
Piano ensemble	93
Two rivers	94
Family tree	95
Waterhole on the Badja	96
The fox at night	97
Moonset 6 a.m.	98
Firelight in the garden	99
At Reedy Creek	100
Red dirt stays	101
Notes	103
Acknowledgements	104

This healing light

Starshine: double vision

'Then we came forth, to see again the stars' – Dante, *Inferno*, Canto 139

When walking by the lake one wintry night
I paused at a bend in the path to watch the lights
from lamps along the bay's farther shore:
I hadn't seen them quite that way before,

like one of van Gogh's painted starry nights.
Although our town is not a place he might
have dreamt: the lake, the quiet little bay,
here were the same reflected lights at play.

I pictured him working, alone beside the Rhône,
his stiff and spattered hands both chilled to the bone.
Saw cobalt, ultramarine and Prussian blues
as I stood there and stared, comparing views.

I've always loved his shining starlit nights
but never thought the real could be as bright.
Now I choose that path whenever I can
and pause, to honour that unhappy man.

His was a troubled life, he died too soon
yet still his brush has lit my scene: no moon
just water, lamps and stars; their sprinkled light
so festive on a frosty cloudless night.

Klimt in the courtyard: woman in gold

Glittering down the tree,
sunlight on the leaves
is a drift of yellow coins,
a work of art to see

as if the slender tree
were a woman dressed in gold
dazzling the soirée
with stylish artistry.

Compositions in a cold climate

A warm reddish glow
from letters on the novel's spine
echoes tassels of a crimson throw
sprawled across the couch.

The daisies' hot yellow
bursts from its blue vase
to meet a scene of autumn willows
within its frame on the wall.

Little brown jugs in a row
on the kitchen dresser shelf,
homely creatures, and slow,
amble along for milking.

Then through a slit of window
bruised and brooding clouds
threaten the room below
that seemed so safe, secure.

Tonal effect, driving home

As day fades to palest grey
I watch the gunmetal road ahead:
under a sullen sky, see pearly lake
and looming over that, a shadow
cast by the humpbacked hill.

Cars flick past, splashing muck.
Around the bend, it's skeleton trees
all lined up along the verge
with each tree stiff, on one leg,
their threadbare arms so cold.

Metaphor

last of evening's light
the lake and I are matched
silver lined with wrinkles

Resurrection

Two men from the museum of warfare
found, at Vignacourt, a wooden chest
saved from the time of the Great War.
It held a cache of glass-plate negatives

now developed, the process filmed:
I watch a man lift dripping prints
from the bath of toxic chemicals
and raise them up to healing light.

One reveals a soldier's ghostly figure:
ninety-six years dead and he's revived,
posed as his hatless, happy-go-lucky self.
In uniform, with one wrist bandaged,

he's safe, for now, behind the lines
but far from certain women he has loved.
Leaning over the back of a chair, he grins
for the *carte postale* he'll write: Dear Mother…

Pictures at a gallery

i I'm over Picasso

His women's eyes fly loose, to cross and veer
away from body parts at war with each other.
Most lips are pursed but vicious teeth will leer
with spite: this gawping girl, which one's her mother?
Is that a bovine lover or guitar,
set beside her tits (or maybe knees)?
Sliced apart, their flesh is angled, hard,
never the flowing form one loves to see –
except, perhaps, below: for there, at the base
is a shallow bowl of grapes, an apple, one pear.
And these have the softer curves of the human face
though only a minor footnote, frugal fare.
Our crowd shuffles along…inspects a clown
with all the charm and fun of a fascist's frown.

ii I recant: the Vollard suite

Pablo I take it all back every word
I love the poetry of your prints
their miracle flowing lines
from frugal cuts in the plate
have pressed the languorous nudes
on paper on memory on the mind
and rhythmic trails of volupté
leave me gasping breathless

Sketch

I'd love to draw your face
with a soft charcoal stick
so every line is marked:
to show where bones lift

the mound of your brow
and where two full lips meet;
when you laugh two dents appear,
there's a furrow from old frowns.

I'd draw your face at night
as it bends above my own:
you are roof and sky, my smiling eye,
my book to read before I sleep.

Millais does Shakespeare in winter

The famous artist used his lissom model
to paint the maid Ophelia on a stream
with willows overhanging all its banks.
He was driven by his vision to begin

but how would he depict the watery scene?
He laid sweet Lizzie Siddal in a bath
with lamps beneath the tub to keep her warm.
Her palms upturned, she floated, fully clothed.

So obsessed was Millais by his task
he quite forgot to notice how time passed.
Five hours flew by and each oil lamp burned out
before he freed his model from her pose.

Drenched and numb, the uncomplaining girl
failed to recover from her long ordeal.
Pneumonia followed; though Millais paid the bills,
a stain remained to shadow her short life.

The drowned Ophelia lives for us today,
her story and her songs still tell the tale
while no one cares for damaged Lizzie now,
that victim of too literal a mind.

Silent film

There was a night when moonrise
filled my summer eyes.
Moved as if by a powerful will,
the full moon came over our hill
until both river and riverside
were lit by its upward glide.

In all that cool white light,
without hesitation or fright,
a small black cat with padded paws
appeared and, making no noise,
nimbly ran down the slope
like an artiste on a tightrope.

I watched, half hidden by trees,
the silent river beside me;
out there, the moon's blank screen
and crossing that, one ink-blot cat; unseen
till now when free to slink and roam
far from the hectic glare of its human home.

A glutton, on reading Szymborska's poems

Her book's as good as a box of sweets
and arrives in the mail as neatly wrapped,
causing squeaks of surprise and glee.
Save them for later, I tell myself,
then lift the lid and look inside –
are their centres the sort I like?
I might try one, or maybe two.

Soon every poem draws me in
and piques my appetite for more.
I savour line after subtle line,
its texture on my tongue, the tang.
By ten o'clock I've eaten the lot.
And better, even, than chocolate,
they'll still be there for another day.

His mother's voice

for John Shaw Neilson

'This peering at lasses is where it begins,
the path that leads to certain sins.

'Whenever you're tempted to stray that way,
fall on your knees, seek the Lord and pray.

'He'll know at once when your thought is lewd.
Nothing escapes the eye of Our Lord.

'He is ever there; all-seeing, above
and only blesses a conjugal love

'so never bring shame upon my head
by touching a woman before you are wed.

'Lascivious thoughts are easy to shun
with your hand on the wheel of work, my son.

'I speak my mind: now woe betide
should one of mine take a girl not his bride.

'And turn your eyes from maids at play
if a wench should even glance your way.'

Natural bigamists

The poet Wordsworth was well served
by amanuensis Dorothy;
discarded mistress (& their daughter);
helpmeet wife & her spinster sister, ministering.

Shelley never lacked for women:
one, a suicide, drowned while bearing their child;
his wife endured her doomed pregnancies;
no scandal ever held him back.

Byron sometimes sodomised women.
He rarely curbed his appetite,
even going so far beyond the pale
as to get his sister with child.

Larkin kept the women loyal but apart:
de facto wife in distant town,
mistress handy in the library,
secretary on the side, convenient.

Turning to recent times, there's Ted.
Sylvia, harassed by children's needs,
seemed too stale and drab; he left
with options A, B, & C, all set to go.

Sylvia's children slept,
snug in crib and cot:
at dawn the girl ran looking, looking…
where her mother was not.

The fatal interruption, imagined

The wretched person from Porlock
arrived with a thunderous knock!
Coleridge leapt from his chair
with a shocked dishevelled air
and stumbled across the floor
to unlock the cottage door.
The fellow presented a bill,
for a bag of spuds, if you will!
He spoke with a southern burr,
a rumble of 'Sir, er, er, Sir…) ·

Sir inhaled the woodbine
his wife had trained to twine
around the cottage door
& down to the sanded floor.
He fumbled in his pocket,
found just a silver locket
torn from her beautiful breast
(along with all the rest)
then opened his mouth to shout
at the lounging slovenly lout:
'D'you know, I was planning a poem
in the peace of this private home?'
'You've driven my words away
So now…I have nothing to say!'

But he went inside to look
for coins in their scullery nook;
and just to placate the oaf,
added some cheese, and a loaf.
Well, that got rid of the fool
with his dusty sack of tools.

A dish of clear creek water
was brought by the neighbour's daughter
and Coleridge doused his head
but the lilting lines had fled.
He tottered back inside:
had the vision really died?
Was it something about towers…
plenteous gardens of flowers?
No use to go and look
for paper, pen and book,
the light had begun to wane
as he scratched his head in vain
and his brain was all awry.
Darkling clouds now swept the sky.

Where two walls meet

The Cross in winter

for Annette Nevin

Making my way along Llankelly Lane
draughty and dark, near dawn, in Darlinghurst,
I wave to derro drinkers easing the pain
of stiffened limbs from nights of cold and thirst.
They're huddled in a niche where two walls meet
to pass around a bottle they must share.
Sunlight slowly trickles down the street.
The café owner yawns but dusts her chairs,
then makes me hot black coffee in a mug
and golden toast that's ripe with melted cheese.
She murmurs local gossip, adds a shrug
and greets the man next door, a Vietnamese
who sips his tea, one eye on the working girls
teetering home to bed on staccato heels.

Change and dismay

Beyond my room comes a scream from some machine
that's tearing up a stretch of broken road
in what has been a shady tree-lined scene;
they'll fill it with apartments, à la mode,
packed in without an inch of space between.
These concrete blocks are bloodless white or grey,
their pebbled yards lack any signs of green
as if such homely relics are passé.
I wonder if the people in the towers
are also grey, like prisoners locked away
in cells, deprived of birds, of grass and flowers
and not allowed to see the light of day.
Will children that they raise be pale and thin
like battery chickens, grown with lives caged in?

Watercolour sketch, Canberra

W.B. Griffin: 'I have planned an ideal city'

I'm waiting near the till in the supermarket queue
behind a dark-skinned girl; we shift impatient feet.
A darker hand, in front, is shuffling paltry coins,
his five- and ten-cent hoard…a white palm waits…
He has enough for fags but not another cent.
The checkout lady sniffs. 'Reckon it's Managed Income!'
Our eyes all slide away to pelting rain outside.

Beneath the sheltering eaves of the chic museum of art
I pass a man on his back, lying across the path.
He's zipped from chin to toe in a grimy sleeping-bag
with a pillow made of rags pushed against the wall.
The face is thin and wan but quite enclosed in sleep.
In the grime of puddled streets he's made his own place
away from want and gusty squalls, tucked in a makeshift bed.

Phasmida the stick-insect woman

She selects my leafy café
where the camouflage is good,
it suits a bone-thin woman
whose limbs are stiff as wood.

Sitting apart, alone,
she eats her lettuce lunch
ignoring those nearby
beneath another branch.

When finished with her coffee
she licks the last few dregs
then, using lanky arms,
assembles whittled legs.

I watch her step away
upright, slow, and stoic
while leaning on those legs
like fragile walking sticks.

Basement blues

This bookshop in a cellar
is dank as a mausoleum:
books of the recent dead
prop stiffly on the shelves
like cattle in a truck.
Some bear faint inscriptions.

Browsing there, I thought I saw
the looming shape of a man
in a cape like a dark shroud
and a black fedora hat.
It was not Aristide Bruant,
nor Hitchcock, in silhouette.
Slowly he prowled along
behind the shelves dividing us –
I could not see his face.

The labyrinthine aisles are clammy cold.
Some bleak, rain-spattered day
I could lose a friend in here
or worse, myself.

Who do you think you are?

The past is a shifting cloud
that tends to elude our grasp.
Hungry arms reach out
and fretful fingertips
scrabble for names and facts:
marriage, death and birth,
who married whom and when?
Towns where people starved
are found to be extinct.
We scan old passenger lists
of ships that brought them away
to a distant alien place
that has become our home.

We think we need to know
if babies were neatly born
in holy wedlock, or out;
if cousins married cousins;
and which ones learned to read.
Was bigamy such a crime
in those unpriested times
or just convenience?
Was Grandma really mad
or only very depressed?
The records are incomplete
and the young, coming on
do not, frankly, give a damn.

Against incineration

I think that they'll be sorry,
historians, the poets
and archaeologists
who cannot dig to reconstruct our lives.

They'll never learn about our habits,
the sorts of illness we endured,
if we're not within the earth,
or not enough of us to supply

a statistician's set.
Bodies lain in soil
can always be exhumed,
the stories in their rotting bones re-read.

To burn a human body
and throw the ash away
seems a callous act,
a wanton waste of evidence.

Old facts will be unlearned,
old lore remain unknown
if we are all dispatched
to basements with their slow, consuming fires.

Country church

The little church at Beloka
compact, sturdy, neat
and built from local stone,
breaks a bare expanse
of empty windswept plains.

Its unexpected spire
adorns a vestibule
beside the southern wall.
I hadn't thought to find
such a church unlocked,

its heavy door ajar
and leading to a porch.
Passing through the grille
to a still and silent place,
I'm slowly overawed

by a once familiar scene:
rows of cedar pews
and hassocks sewn by hand,
stained glass and prayer-books,
a threadbare carpet strip.

The steadfast country church
has kept the founders' pledge.
It nearly revives a need
to fall on my knees and pray –
but I have lost the key.

Dead flies have been trapped

in the small stone house, set on a track
dug from the barren side of a hill
a woebegone window gazes out
beyond the spidered, cobwebbed sill.

Waiting, alert, and willingly watching,
once, the glass was dressed in lace,
a delicate pattern of roses and leaves
that never wholly covered its face.

Their friend would come with a billy of cream
for the treats of occasional afternoon teas
and the curtains seemed to smile at cups
balanced, uneasy, on decorous knees.

These wintry days there's an air of despair
with never the sound of a cheerful knock
from the friend, in boots, who limped to the door,
a door that, now, is always locked.

With eyelets clotted by silting dust,
the fine old lace is frayed and split
but allows a glimpse of darkness within:
though drawn, the curtains have left a slit.

And still the patient window stares
down the slope of the tussocked hill
past rusting galvo and broken wire:
he neither comes, nor ever will.

The visitor eats, New Year's Eve

He's hunched over his plate at the table,
Eyes lowered to fork up food
And arms curved in as if guarding his grub.
Other guests stand about, busy drinking.

It's a long drive down the mountain
but life back home has soured.
He risks a glance at the party, still chatting,
then ducks to avoid a curious eye.

Meat, he takes, and potatoes, savoury eggs.
Each is shovelled in, chewed and gulped
before the thin brown hand reaches again
(avoiding flummeries and sweets).

On this last night of the old year
he's glad to forget the old shack
where oats are a staple, day in, day out.
Oats and heroic silence; the dog died.

Happy? Why would you be?

I was sorry to see the old year go
like a foreign friend I'd come to know.

It had lost the power to worry me,
I'd lived it through and survived, you see.

While a new year fills some folk with joy
who greet each one like a brand new toy,

I feel its approach as a hovering threat
or a knock at my door concerning a debt.

Worse is the thought of more new years,
bringing along their hints and tears,

for one will carry on its back
a portent in a heavy sack:

unpleasant news designed for me.
I fear the year I can't foresee.

True minds

True minds

Oh, there was no impediment at all
when you observed, inquired, and searched for me,
joking with my friends in the lecture hall.
Just then I was footloose and fancy free,
thus well equipped for study of your charms:
watching your lips, so mobile, warm and full,
I somehow sensed I'd never come to harm.
What's more, you had this winning trick, a playful
way of singing suitable bits of song
at any time of day or moonlit night.
That spring, when side by side we walked along
a river track with the bluest hills in sight,
I knew the time had come to see if we
could prove the worth of love's slow chemistry.

A man

He's worked the shifts in quarries and pits
up north, at forty degrees; long days
with older men, shovelling clay.

Now he's an intellectual
with a beard around the rim of his jaw.
'Love it,' I said and touched it with awe.

This summer he's on a removals van,
lifting and shifting pianos and stuff.
He's strong enough but tender, not rough.

When I met him after work today
sweat was a stain on the back of his shirt.
The scent of sweat on a man never hurt –

this one's for real, true as blue steel;
he left the bush to travel south
and I want the taste of his mouth.

In praise of easy days

We loved ourselves
when we were young.
You seemed urbane
and so well hung.

You liked the little
scarves I wore
and when we danced
around the floor

you held me tight.
I watched your eyes
for you were hot
and worldly-wise:

you knew some tricks
which I did not
but I was quick
and learned a lot.

A correspondence

Oh, Love, send me letters, languid and long
for I dream of the days we dawdled abroad,
sultry in shorts and a slinky sarong.

You'd wheedle and whisper you wanted a rest
then lie on the lawn and loosen your belt
while murmuring words I could never resist

so I'd cast off my clothes and consent to *l'amour*…
But love in a letter lacks the allure.
Our summers were sweeter; far sweeter, for sure.

Aimez-vous Chekhov?

Leaving a film of *The Duel*,
we link arms and talk about
the Russian author, what
he meant to us years ago.

Back then, we lay by a river
and you put the question,
'Who's your favourite writer?'
Silly question, I thought,

and answered slowly,
sensing a lot was at stake.
'So many favourites,' I said.
'But I love my Chekhov's *Tales*.'

At once I knew I'd scored.
You opened blue eyes wide,
surprised and quite impressed.
I smiled, pleased, a little smug.

You spoke of Hemingway and Scott.
What you didn't say,
and I only learned tonight,
was how many hours at school

you'd spent alone in the library
while other boys were away.
Deep in a leather chair you read
the whole entire works of A.P. Chekhov.

Sonnet for the second thought

with thanks to Shakespeare

My lover's eyes are nothing like dark pools,
they're more like water, grey with greasy suds.
Observing sexy girls he tends to drool
as cattle do, when paused in munching cud.
His hair is also grey, think scouring pad
though rather sparser than it used to be.
I don't suggest the man's a faithless cad,
he's stayed the course; is living, still, with me.
A drinking mate of his who longs to stray
will ogle girls, from bar to boozy bar,
hoping to pick one up along the way
and court her with his sporty low-slung car.
My love's at home; he's cooking me a meal
I reckon he's by far the better deal.

Refuge

A woven blanket wraps me round –
warmth of touch, of sight and sound,

from songs as you work at the kitchen sink;
you telling me plainly what you think,

again; a rustle of pages while you read;
the rock of your knee within the bed;

the merest snuffle as you sleep;
your chest as refuge when I weep;

two old brown shoes, parked on the mat,
what could be more reassuring than that?

The haircut

I felt especially honoured
when allowed, this once,
to take a pair of scissors
and ever so timidly
trim some silver curls
from your beloved head.

I snipped a few tufts
to even up the back
then stopped, afraid to go
beyond the bounds
of what was allowed.
Zeal was inappropriate.

After I'd swept them up,
this clump of fallen tendrils,
and thrown them in the bin,
I thought to myself, perhaps
I should have kept a few,
saved them for remembrance.

Edge

In the sleepy midday quiet of the living room
I hear an intermittent murmur; a mutter.
A gale's got under the heel of the front door,
making a quiet rumble, nothing more.

The door speaks of how it's set between
my time inside the house and the world out there;
how a green and lifeless thing's become the portal
of our days, has witnessed so much family lore

for thirty years. The slam of this wooden slab
signals my darling is home from the lakes and safe.
As a final chore each night he locks, before
striding down the darkened corridor

to me, reading late in the great warm bed.
We lie together, twinned in sleep, until
eager for news, I creep to open our door
and read the morning sky for what it holds in store.

Something is about to happen

From outside the front door
comes the rattle of keys –
a silence falls, prolonged…

cries of corella and crow.
Overhead, a helicopter's heart
thuds as it ferries pain

and our whole house trembles.
Then you step inside, smile,
and I am in your arms again.

Creature comforts

Nothing's as warm in my hand
as my old black fountain pen
moving across a page;

no silk as soft to touch
as the slender foot of a child
as I smooth on healing oil;

no sight so thrusting bright
on a grey denuded twig
as a scarlet robin's breast;

and nothing as welcome as warmth
from a fire of salvaged wood
thawing frozen feet.

The best surprise at dusk
is a wombat nosing her way
down the slope for a drink.

The neatest pattern I know
is seven crested pigeons
nestled in our lawn

and no other sound as dear
in the quiet of the night
as your whisper in my ear.

Signs of life

i Extrasensory

With you alive, so utterly here,
not close at hand but somewhere near
I sense you're in the house with me;
I don't need to touch your hand or see
you pause and spin your office chair,
hear a swish as you brush your hair
or pad barefoot across the floor
to a noiseless sliding door.
I read each signal that denotes
your thought; with clearings of the throat
they make a wave, speak of your presence,
and even suggest a scent, your essence.
Intimations are all l need,
rich companionship indeed.

ii Dead silence

Alone in the house, awake at night,
the place feels eerie; even the light
is odd and seems to be alien, cold.
I check the locks: they may not hold.
When floors release the slightest creak
I peer downstairs, rehearse a shriek
then dare, 'Who's there?'… I do not cry.
The dry old wood makes no reply.
No friend calls up on the faithless phone.
The house is like uncaring stone,
it neither helps nor lends an ear.
My sleep is haunted, morbid, queer,
for in the silence I've come to fear
an unhealthy breath is drawing near.

Summertime

Birds chime with the sound
of your voice at the piano…
cool air blows around my feet
as I paint the toenails festive red.

At night you play my favourite tunes
but when you come to 'Green Fields',
my problem is, how can I contrive
to do two things at once?

I want to lounge and listen
while also rising from the couch
to move into your arms and dance,
sway with you, even as you play.

When we're sleeping, skin on skin,
with your mouth so near at hand,
the waves of your breath
come falling, falling on my bare arm.

The gift

Late on Christmas Eve
at the river, by moonlight
you caught a fine fat trout:
brown, with rosy freckles.
I watched as you thwacked it.
Thwacked and thwacked
against a low stone wall
until it was fully dead.

Next day was still Christmas.
We found an old fireplace
where you wrapped the trout
in a parcel of tinselly foil
and cooked it with tender care
then eased a blade along the spine
and fed me soft pink flesh –
I ate slowly, thinking of the scene last night.

The red chalk drawing

Thus, in a thousand years all men shall see
How beautiful you were, how I was faint
And yet how wise I was in loving you.
– Michelangelo, Sonnet xvii

As they made love that afternoon
she felt his body become
the drawing by Michelangelo
of the nude, in red chalk,
with long curving muscles
in bottom, belly and back.

It seemed as if she held
the image in her arms –
how else to comprehend
the form of the greatest art
so surely, in secret,
if not by holding him?

The male buttock
is taut like a rock
but smooth in the hand
and rounded, warm,
packed with energy;
not cold like marble or stone.

The old way of looking
was somehow incomplete
whereas now she possessed
the chalk drawing fully
as she did him,
with all five senses.

Lament

'We will miss ourselves when we die' – Alex Skovron, 'Imperium'

Thinking, tonight, of all the books we've read
you and I, together late at night,
I know we'll miss ourselves when we are dead.

Might even miss the tears I've sometimes shed
while waiting for a sign of early light
to search among the books that we have read

for words that would relieve my nagging dread.
A life with books has made us erudite.
I know we'll miss ourselves when we are dead,

miss secrets whispered side by side in bed
arousing sudden laughter and delight.
Thinking, tonight, of all the books we've read

arranged along a stranger's shelves instead,
fills me again with shrinking icy fright –
I know we'll miss ourselves when we are dead,

cut off from everything the poets said
in lines you learned when young and still recite.
Thinking, tonight, of all the books we've read,
I know we'll miss ourselves when we are dead.

Watchers

In two minds

It's three a.m. and black as pitch
when the minds in my head begin a fight
that tosses me from side to side.
The stern one dreads the day ahead,
reviews a list of pressing tasks,
invokes embarrassment,
smart retorts I failed to make,
anxiety for friends at risk.

My dreaming mind will show a film
whenever it can seize the chance:
troupes of actors fill the screen
in fleeting guest appearances.
The themes are often quite obscure
with little shape but lively scenes:
riddling symbols come and go
before I work out what they mean.

After all, I'm here to rest…
Just when the action's warming up
my other mind butts in: a switch
is flicked, the movie fades
and hordes of morbid moods descend.
Exhausted by the night, I rise
at five to face the wait for light
and all the dross of radio news.

A reverie

'After such knowledge, what forgiveness?' – T.S. Eliot, 'Gerontion'

Today, the queerest waking dream.
Like any normal dream, it seems:
my dad looks into my childhood room
at dusk, a sort of sultry gloom.

Wringing his hands, he shakes his head
at my mother's body on the bed.
She is, by now, just three days dead,
his face becomes a mottled red.

Why did she choose my room to lie
in, drug herself and die?
'Look what I've done to you,' he intones.
I want remorse; more tears, a moan.

He went; then I sat up; I knew
the words in this odd rendezvous
were never said by him; too bad.
It's just… I wish he had.

The temptation

I hope I'll never try
to imitate my mother's way of death:
her low despairing cry,

perhaps a choking; a leaving behind of breath
to sink on hard pillows
and become a thing changed, like nothing on earth;

her cold room in an odd way hollow
when she failed to rouse or react.
Hope I don't use pills like those she swallowed

to hurt the one who broke their pact,
who was stopped in his tracks at her door
by the undeniable fact:

no gunshot wound, no blood on the floor,
only the terrible odour of absence –
then words ringing, iron on stone, when he swore.

Wishful Thinking

The lame girl wakes from dreams
of running along a beach,
running to tall red cliffs
so far beyond the reach
of swollen, twisted feet.

The blind man's dreaming too–
of his beloved's face
but he can only try
with fumbling hands to trace
its smoothly curving lines.

My early morning dream
is what I could have said
to my despairing mother,
alone and restless in her bed,
and me so far away.

After fifty years

Will my rosebush ever wake up?
I pause, stand before it and stare –
grey stalk limbs: austere, unlovely
and non-committal, giving no hint.
Beneath the bush are knotted roots
bearing the faint mark of my mother
whose shaky hands once pressed them down
deep into loose and soothing soil.

Spring after spring, the roses have come,
luscious, red-gold, with the scent of peach.
Lately, only a few made the journey
and each one struggled, puny and weak,
swaying on thorn-encrusted limbs
so dry and scarecrow-spare: still, I watch…
but the bush is adamant, as if to say
'You ask too much, too much of me.'

Closing the gap

for Rosie, again

It was only a dreary city street –
I ducked and weaved through lunchtime crowds
searching for two I longed to see.

At last you walked through an open door,
a man in a shirt undone at the throat.
Our eyes lit up and we both dashed forward.

With luck, our friend was behind you, too.
She waved to me and quickened her pace
we were running, running, to mend the breach,

restore a closeness broken off.
When we finally met in that hectic place
we flung out our arms in healing embrace,

certain we'd never be parted again.
A wind blew papers round our feet
and a bus rumbled by on its mundane route
but we were an island: quiet, complete.

Watchers

Behind my flat is a house with a 'stage',
an upstairs balcony built on the back,
and there sits a woman of advanced age.

The balcony rail obscures her face,
above is white hair; below, crossed legs.
One arm has a kind of careful grace

as it rises and falls, rises and falls,
lifting a cup or the cigarette.
Often she stands against the wall

and I feel exposed, down here in the gloom,
behind the tilted slats of my blind:
her glance invades my private room.

I build her story from bits I know.
The trek out here from Budapest,
a war of seventy years ago;

her girlhood in hiding, isolation,
the cold and damp of underground
ill lit; a fear of slow starvation

that stunts the growth and learning too.
Schools were closed to girls like her
and down in the cellar friends were few.

Here she exists in an alien place.
I keep an eye: she goes in, comes out,
alone with the sun, the sky, so much space.

The fragrance of lemons

for Sarah Colquhoun

I loved the Meyer lemon tree
planted by my neighbour friend,
a lively woman, vivacious and kind.
She'd squeezed it into a space between
her cobbled path and the old brick wall.

It only began to bear good crops
after Laura moved away:
I missed our daily talks at the gate.
A series of owners came and went
as the tree began to reach for the sun.

I learned too late that Laura had died
but our blue connecting gate remained
and sometimes I pilfered fallen fruit:
the lemons were sweet and full of juice,
with skin a clear unspotted yellow.

The latest man to buy the house
uprooted her white oleander hedge
and all the secret English bulbs
she'd set to flower in spring.
Only the lemon tree stood its ground

in a place with the look of a wrecker's yard.
I'd rescue fruit from lopped-off branches
left where they'd fallen against the wall
then stealthily nurse the lemons home,
my apron cradling the precious load.

The owner seemed to be pruning the tree,
I never dreamt he'd take it down.
One day I opened our old blue gate
and my breath stopped: I knew it before
I saw the heap of mangled limbs.

The wreck of a woman's dream, they lay
across the broken cobbled path.
I stood in falling rain and stared:
the fruit was blotched with a fetid mould
sodden, pale, and cold to touch.

The silence

He makes me laugh.
I'm slamming saucepans down
in full-blown cranky rant
when he cuts in fast
with best falsetto mimicry
that takes the wind
right out of my sails.
'I really *mean* it,' I shout.

On he goes, undeterred,
taking the mickey –
pitch-perfect plummy tone,
'Lah di dah, lah di dah…'
until, punctured, I fall
on the couch, gulping air
and gasping on his gags.
He revs it up; I writhe.

Miss Bickers next door
raises an eyebrow.
'Volatile!' she tartly remarks,
remarks to herself
while feeding the bird.
She never hears the sequel.
What follows in the silence
is no one else's business.

Zara going home

She brought two roses to my bed:
one, a bud, and bluish pink,
the other, white, almost a posy.
Setting the vase beside my head
she said, 'Sad. I'm leaving.
'You keep these instead.'

Her mind was full of ideas,
songs to write, scenes to draw,
ideas of such intensity,
like currents under restless seas,
they swirled inside her mind.
Soothed by roses, I dreamt, at ease.

Your roses

for Lesley Masur

When the clatter of things
leaves me alone
I listen to your roses
whisper advice.
They speak of the scent of rain
on dampened soil,
of wrens preening wings.
Your roses bring these inside.

Quiet, I hear their voices.
When I forget,
and waste my days
in bustle and haste,
I see them droop
with a faint murmur
there, in the crystal vase,
upright on our window ledge.

A breeze stirs the curtains
and they remind me…
soon, petal by petal,
your roses will leave me.

Interwoven

for M.K.

It's not a scarf I often dare to wear:
a little like some cleric's stole, it hangs,
red run through with gold, down the back
of my worn and rather faded blue armchair.

The scarf is never lent or even moved,
coming, as it did, from another world,
mailed by you as a special birthday gift
and murmuring in its folds that I was loved.

These winter days, in the arms of the old blue chair
I gather warmth from sunlight streaming in
through walls of glass; and settled, reading, there
I sense your quiet presence in bright air.

The fever suite

i a bed of one's own

There's much to be said
for sleeping alone:
the reading lamp's on
till way past midnight,
again when I wake at dawn
& it's my hand on the radio switch.

Stretching across the Vacant Side
is a rare expanse of luxurious space:
for the phone, on hand for private chats,
for books and papers, lazily stacked.
There's even my mini writing desk.
What more would an ailing woman want?

The curtains are open for nature study,
a voyeur's look at the local birds:
rosellas kiss while pigeons snooze,
today I saw two gang-gangs mate, twice.
I've half a mind to fake my state
& loll in bed for a hundred days.

ii generation of memoranda

Ideas arise from Inner Self:
Outer Self, steno-sec, takes notes.
Imperative to shift paperwork
accumulated on Vacant Side.
Sundry items to be filed in study,
en route to bathroom or fridge.

Within Self a nervous tic jumps:
unfiled notes might be sucked
into vacuum cleaner's maw; or
confused with used tissue & flushed.
Or be sent to persons other than Self,
causing muddle, alarm, affront.

My dressing table & divers desks
assume a patchwork look
as small inscribed squares of paper
settle under sullen dust.
In draughts, some flit as moths
to realms undreamt of.
I can't lift a finger to prevent it.

Suspended

My other normal life
is now a faded dress
on a bent wire coat hanger
hooked on the curtain rod.

I lie below in a restless bed,
too weak to weigh up loves and losses
or tidy a desk distraught with tasks.
I've just enough will to gaze

when a biff of breeze enters, left,
and the old beloved life
slumps on the shoulder
of the cold metal hanger:

in one silent shiver
it slides to the floor, inert,
a remnant of red poppies
on a field of crumpled wheat.

For want of a spoon

Endgame

Dead is one thing.
Sad, I guess,
but dying is hard,
prolonged duress.

No quick cutting off
like tying a knot
just pain to repel,
brave or not.

Night watch

I heard the owl
upon our hill
I heard the groaning night
grow still.
I tossed and sank
in fevered sheets

and feather pillow
turned to stone.
In dreams you came to me again
although I was alone:
my opened eyes saw nothing
but the window's empty stare.

A silver teaspoon

For want of a spoon
she bent too low,

for want of sight
she fell on her wrist,

for want of strength
she snapped the wrist.

For want of a wrist
she lost what it takes,

for want of that
she lost her home,

for want of home
she lost her will

and wanting will,
she lost her wits

all for the sake
of a little silver spoon.

The force

The earth is exerting a force, its right to claim our mother.
One night it brings her down: she crawls, gives up, lies there,
a tiny heap of crumpled woman. Unfound but not unwanted.

Only at dawn do people hear her faint and plaintive bell.
They gather her up and rush her off to hospital.
She learns the strength to totter. But still, it wants her down

and will not be deterred. When she stumbles, unaware
beside a traitorous stove that gashes neck and thigh,
we help her find unsteady feet. The earth is prepared to wait.

It is there on the off-chance, observing this very old lady,
a mere wisp of tissue paper. Next time, it is clear,
she will be no match for the pull of the earth.

He was an entertainment

for John Rosewell

Sometimes we never know
how thoroughly we loved a man
until we hear he's breathed his last.

Reading your words about his end
I cried and could not stop.
I mourned the time in our shared past

of reckless salad days
when we four made our playful way
through learning, laughter, lust.

These now begin to have the look
of faded relics gathering dust.

A hundred times

At Grandpa's dinner table,
no talking during meals
and chew your food 100 times.
No staring when your Grandpa licks

each meticulous thumb
to mop up errant crumbs
on a dainty bread-and-butter plate.
Think of all the starving children…

Ignore the serviette
as he launders a wobbling lip
or hurrumphs a rumbly throat before
taking a sip from the crystal glass.

Though I chewed faster than him
no one shifted her chair
to rise and leave the dining room
until he signed that he was done.

A popular song, 1930s

for Kathleen White

Back then, no boys made passes at girls
in glasses & never at those who wore boots.

When other girls wore pointy shoes
cut low to show their ankles off
her twisted feet were locked in boots
laced up the front.

As she limped about, the butt of smirks,
a popular song burned her ears:
'Boots, boots, boots, boots,
'Movin' up and down again!'

After a surgeon's knife on bone,
pain, and the wait for brand-new shoes,
sensible lace-ups, 'nigger brown'.
No slingbacks or peep-toes, but proper shoes.

Today she'd have the last laugh
as carefree girls in high-heeled boots
of patent leather and sexy suede
teeter down exacting streets.

Water sleekly falls

Sun on my back

The early river, with rising mist:
a pelican skims along the surface
and flocks of wood ducks swoon on pools.
They make a pattern of formal grace.

Free at last from the frost of night,
robins cling to the sides of trees
and scan for worms in the soil below
then pounce and grab with practised ease.

The river belongs to them and to me,
sitting beside a rutted track;
no cars, no blokes on motorbikes,
just the bush, and ripples of birdsong.

Bush walk

The mountain path is too severe
and more grey tors come into view
so I stop my trudge from rock to rock
and veer away through wattle scrub
to a stand of granite boulders.
From dark, half-hidden burrows
the wombat trails go winding down
to a gully that's narrow and steep.

Here, all light in a twist of water sleekly falls,
rim over rim: quiet, seamless, scintillant.

Reflections, Jerrabomberra

The blue-grey heron
stalks along, level with me
but keeping a distance.
It steps with quiet intent,
prodding slits between the reeds
that fringe these shallow pools.

Prowling under the trees,
I also take great care,
warily placing each foot
so as not to snap a twig,
and peering up, through leaves,
for coloured wings that flick.

The Chigaree

A cheeping thornbill on the lawn
with sunlight-buttered rump
sings to welcome signs of dawn
as cheerful birds will do

but he is more the subtle sleuth
that twitches stalks apart,
investigating cryptic earth
in a beetling underworld.

Arrested by a skilful tweak,
insects meet their end
caught in a ruthless thornbill's beak
and never seen again.

Piano ensemble

These magpies on the windowsill
are our familiar birds
and listen when my husband plays
a song with lilting chords.

One of them, old Bing by name,
who loves a smoochy tune,
fluffs his feathers into a ruff
as if about to croon.

Instead he drops a glistening plop
from coyly lowered bum
then warbles off a bar or two,
a sort of magpie hum.

Two rivers

Mourning, here, by Molonglo,
its thistled banks and swamps,
I search through darker depths
for a lost water-colour world,

a place where all birds sang
and only jersey cows intruded;
a willowy green space
framed by the tallest gums.

We'd walk a winding path
past the small stone house,
hollyhocks, roses, a grassy
slope down to the last gate.

Unlatch and run to the river's bank
with the red wooden dinghy.
It was a place, always summer,
where the parents never quarrelled;

where my dad made time
to teach me how to row
in narrow tricky Onkaparinga.
Once launched on the water,

we reached for blackberries
ripe and black, oozing juice.
Fat yabbies nibbled our bait
that swayed in the river's flow.

This cool translucent green
gave every pebble colour,
gave ferns a freckled shade…
We always stayed till the light had gone.

Family tree

In the scarlet storm of a fire
a towering gum tree sank
on weakened thighs.
The belly was ripped apart

to leave a gaping hole,
the crown and every branch
vanished into ash:
a headless torso remains.

Close against the gum
is one whose lower limbs
are wrapped around the source
like a mother's clinging child.

This other, younger tree
has grown up tall and strong.
Its smooth and speckled branches
are clothed in freshest green

that forms a canopy,
a new and noisy world
alive with breeding birds
fighting each other for food.

Waterhole on the Badja

for Moya Pacey

The pool in the gorge is a secret place
you'd never, before, allowed me to see.
Ignoring advice, I dived and swam,
as perfectly happy as I could be.

Crossing the river's cool dark pool,
at last I achieved my summer dream,
swimming slowly with silent strokes.
You were high on a rock above the stream.

I sensed you were only casting a line,
pretending to fish for rainbow trout
while keeping watch, for fear of snakes,
and really wishing I'd come right out.

Then I saw its narrow head,
sharp as a pencil and aiming for me.
The snake was fast but I was faster…
You were right to be wary, I have to agree.

The fox at night

Padding across the frosty grass
she alerted our security light
then, nimble as a dancer,
sprang up to an old blue bench
under the kitchen window.
With two intrusive paws
balanced on the sill
she watched our pallid faces.

A fox in the garden's a pest,
an unwanted visitant,
but her tawny fur was sleek
and the focused, amber eyes
most curious and bold.
Healthy she seemed, to us,
but full of all the sense
of sharp animal greed.

For a moment, we loved her
at midnight, under a full moon.

Moonset 6 a.m.

This morning on the porch
I had the luck to lift my eyes:
swooning there in cloudless skies
was a coloured moon, the sun's twin
and stained with the same blood-orange tones.
Slipping down from a great height,
it met the mountains' rim of blue
and roused the moths of the western plains.

Firelight in the garden

The fireplace in our garden
has acquired a sacred air

since my father built it there
under sheltering gums;

the fallen twigs and branches
build our cooking fires.

Old bricks are loose and leaning,
as if they crave more heat

but the frugal little fireplace
still feeds the family's feasts.

Sizzling racks of lamb
and a billy boiled for tea

make fine sustaining meals
on crisp autumnal nights

while smoky in the shadows
drifts a ghost whose gift it was.

At Reedy Creek

A cluster of reeds is combed by the current's whirl
as if the greenish reeds are being rinsed
by the slender cleansing hands of a salon girl.
The creek flows clear and quick; it has done since
the summer rain, and the coiffed reeds sway.
Stripping, then tying back my tangled hair,
I dive in deep to find the bed of clay.
It's slippery-smooth to hold so I work with care,
digging out the lumps of precious stuff.
Arranging the clay along the bank, I knead
it into rounded forms: when set in a rough
design, they soon resemble loaves of bread
but little loaves, all bluish-grey and white,
dense and luminous in the watery light.

Red dirt stays

I like the way it insinuates:
between the toes, in nails and hair,
the shirts we wear, our skin,
leaving a stubborn red grin.
How, in the semi-arid lands
it chimes with red-winged parrots,
and the glint of a scarlet gash
on the breasts of mistletoe birds.
Red is there in dry creek beds
and in the banks of verges,
making walls for mating birds
urged by the wet to breed:
kingfisher, pardalote, rainbow-bird
drill their nest burrows in.

Red bakes hard in the Centre,
held by saltbush and spinifex.
It's under lakes with salt-crust rims,
on the bleached bones of frail birds,
relic skulls of defeated beasts
and egg-white shells of shrivelled snails.
It's found on the rusty face
of cliffs above the turquoise seas
in easy curving bays; in caves
it's saving certain secrets
left from former days.
Iron-willed in ironstone rocks,
its bony fingers reach and lock,
supervising soft white sand.

Tamed and watered, red dirt feeds
the green groves of mango trees.
And after storms it settles down
in the grooves on iron roofs
of dying country towns:
against their haywire fences,
on tired walls of shuttered shops.
In the long lonely gutters
and sad forgotten churches
red dirt stays.
It smokes on the rims of our wheels
and spins off narrow tracks
scarred and cut with ruts.
Even now, it's painted on my inner eye.

Notes

van Gogh, Vincent, painting: *Starry Night over the Rhone*, 1888: see Mark Roskill ed., *The Letters of Vincent van Gogh*, Fontana Paperbacks 1982.

Dante, Alighieri, *Inferno*, translated by Robert & Jean Hollander. Anchor Books, New York 2002.

The Sonnets of Michelangelo, translated by Elizabeth Jennings, Allison & Busby, London 1969.

Eliot, T.S., 'Gerontion' in *Collected Poems 1909–1935*, Faber & Faber Ltd 1958.

Acknowledgements

Many poems in *Catching the Light* have been published in the following publications: Mark Tredinnick ed., *Australian Love Poems*, Inkerman & Blunt, 2013; Geoff Page ed., *Best Australian Poems*, Black Inc., 2015; Lawson, Wright & Blaney-Murphy eds, *The Way to the Well*, Central Coast Poets Inc., 2014; Ann Nadge ed., *First Refuge*, Ginninderra Press 2016; Edgar, Kituai, Renew & Hall eds, *Flood, Fire & Drought*, Ginninderra Press, 2016.

They have also appeared in the following newspapers & periodicals: *The Weekend Australian*; *Canberra Times*; *Quadrant*; *Meanjin* (see Joe Dolce, *Dirty Laundry: The Art of Confessional Writing*, December 2017; *Antipodes*.

And they have been read at The University of Adelaide; Poetry at the House, ANU; Manning Clark House; The Salt Room, Gorman House Arts Centre; and Smith's Alternative, Canberra.

www.ingramcontent.com/pod-product-compliance
Lightning Source LLC
Chambersburg PA
CBHW070102120526
44589CB00033B/1550